EDGE
BOOKS™

SANITATION
INVESTIGATION

GARBAGE, WASTE, DUMPS, AND YOU

The Disgusting Story Behind What We Leave Behind

by CONNIE COLWELL MILLER

Consultant:
Robert Janus
Planterra Management Ltd.
Victoria, British Columbia

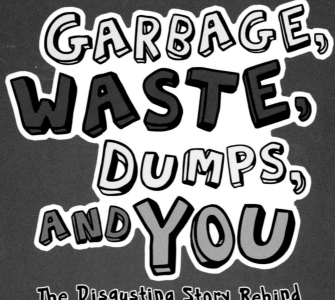

Capstone

Mankato, Minnesota

Edge Books are published by Capstone Press,
151 Good Counsel Drive, P.O. Box 669, Mankato, Minnesota 56002.
www.capstonepress.com

Library of Congress Cataloging-in-Publication Data
Miller, Connie Colwell, 1976–
    Garbage, waste, dumps, and you: the disgusting story behind what we leave
behind / by Connie Colwell Miller.
    p. cm. — (Edge books. Sanitation investigation)
    Includes bibliographical references and index.
    ISBN-13: 978-1-4296-1996-7 (hardcover)
    ISBN-10: 1-4296-1996-1 (hardcover)
    1. Refuse and refuse disposal — Juvenile literature. I. Title. II. Series.
TD792.M553 2009
628.4'4 — dc22   2008000535

Summary: Describes the history of waste removal and the current waste
removal system.

Editorial Credits
Mandy Robbins, editor; Alison Thiele, designer; Wanda Winch, photo researcher;
    Sarah L. Schuette, photo shoot direction; Marcy Morin, scheduler

Photo Credits
Alamy/Arco Images/ O. Diez, 22
Can Stock Photo, 27
Capstone Press/Karon Dubke, cover, 1, 4, 18, 28–29
Getty Images Inc./Hulton Archive/Jacob A. Riis, 8; The Image Bank/Thomas
    Schmitt, 12; Justin Sullivan, 19; Photographer's Choice/Stuart McCall, 24;
    Time & Life Pictures/Alfred Eisenstaedt, 14–15
Houserstock/Pilar Law, 10
iStockphoto/Alistair Forrester, 7; Ralph125, 21; tomba, 16
Shutterstock/clearviewstock (yellow hazard stripes on road), 6, 23; David
    Huntley (push pin), 5, 13, 20, 29; Gavin Cooper (cardboard design
    element), all; Gilmanshin (grunge background element), all; Larisa
    Lofitskaya (sheet of paper with torn edges), 6, 23; Tyler Boyes, cover (tile
    floor in background)
SuperStock Inc./Image Asset Management, Ltd., 11

1 2 3 4 5 6 13 12 11 10 09 08

TABLE OF CONTENTS

Chapter 1

GETTING TO KNOW YOUR GARBAGE

About 12 percent of the trash that Americans generate consists of food scraps.

Moldy leftovers, empty pizza boxes, and plastic wrap. Soggy paper cups, snotty tissues, and food packaging. Most people in the United States produce about 4 pounds (1.8 kilograms) of this stuff every day. We call it garbage.

Most people toss their garbage in the trash without thinking twice. Once a week, they put the garbage bin on the curb for the garbage truck. Then they're done with it. But is that the whole story?

EDGE FACT:

About one third of the garbage that Americans throw away is packaging.

TRASH-SAVVY

It's a good idea to get to know your city's rules for trash disposal. Some cities have limits on how much trash you can throw away each week. Sanitation workers may pick up only one trash bin or dumpster full of garbage per week.

Some cities allow you to pay for removal of extra trash. You buy stickers to place on your extra bags of trash. The stickers tell sanitation workers that it's okay for them to pick up extra bags. The money from your purchase helps pay for the costs of removing the extra garbage.

Some people burn trash in fire pits. But burning trash can release poisonous fumes into the air. In some cities, burning trash is illegal. It's probably best to fork over the cash for proper garbage removal.

Ash from burning garbage can leave dangerous chemicals in the soil.

What do you think happens to your garbage after it's put on that truck? Where does it go? Does it get turned into anything else? And what do you think would happen if we didn't have a system for removing our garbage? Would the trash just pile up around us? Would it eventually break down and go away? And what would happen to the earth?

Chapter 2
TIME LINE OF TRASH

In the early 1900s, people living in poor areas of New York City left garbage outside their homes.

LEARN ABOUT:
- Ditching and dumping
- Plagues
- Sanitation solutions

Getting rid of trash has been a problem for people since ancient times. People have always had old clothing, food remains, and other waste to dispose of. In the past, people got rid of trash by simply throwing it outside. Today, people care more about what garbage does to the planet.

Ditch It!

Thousands of years ago, people threw waste outside their homes. That practice continued until the 1700s. Some people threw waste out their windows. Others dumped it into nearby waterways. Leftover stew? Out the window with a splash. Spoiled milk? Into the sea it goes.

These were not very responsible ways to get rid of waste. City streets were often overrun with garbage. Waste dirtied the water supplies. Rats populated the cities and spread germs. People got sick and died.

Ancient Garbage Dumps

Around 500 BC, the ancient Greeks came up with a way to keep their cities clean. They began piling garbage outside their cities in big heaps called dumps. To keep the smell out, dumps were at least 1 mile (1.6 kilometers) from the city. The Romans developed a similar system about 500 years later.

Unfortunately, when the Greek and Roman civilizations died out, the dumps did too. People around the world continued throwing waste outside or into waterways.

Remains of Greek buildings still stand. Luckily, the garbage dumps have rotted away.

Millions of people who died of plagues were buried in mass graves.

Deadly Sicknesses

From the 1300s to the 1700s, a series of deadly diseases infected people around the world. Millions of people died from these **plagues**. Most scientists agreed that the illnesses were caused by filthy living conditions.

At last, people started looking for better ways to get rid of waste. In the mid-1700s, people in Europe and the United States began dumping their garbage in small valleys and other low-lying areas.

plague — a serious disease that affects many people, spreads quickly, and often causes death

Incinerator smokestacks often tower over surrounding buildings.

Burn, Baby, Burn!

People using the first dumps discovered something interesting. The garbage in the dumps would occasionally burst into flames.

Scientists learned that the mix of rotting waste made a chemical called methane. Methane is dangerous, and the explosions it caused were dangerous too. But something good came from these explosions. People noticed that burning waste turned the garbage to ash. That meant less garbage!

This discovery led to the building of the first **incinerators** in the 1870s. People used these machines to burn garbage. In cities without incinerators, workers often lit dumps on fire to reduce the amount of garbage.

EDGE FACT:

Governments monitor incinerators because burning garbage can create toxic chemicals.

incinerator — a furnace for burning garbage

Keeping Clean

In the 1900s, people made laws about how to get rid of waste. **Hazardous waste** had to be disposed of safely. People could no longer dump waste in bodies of water. Cities started waste removal programs to pick up garbage regularly and put it in dumps.

From these beginnings, our modern waste management system developed. Most people agree that we have more work to do. But we sure have come a long way from throwing slop into the streets!

hazardous waste — materials that contain harmful chemicals

Chapter 3

TRASH TODAY

Mechanical arms on garbage trucks make trash collection a cleaner job for sanitation workers.

Today, not all of our waste is handled in the same way. About one-third of U.S. waste is **recycled** or **composted**. Recycling breaks down materials and uses them to make new items. Composting turns waste such as food scraps and yard cuttings into valuable soil or fertilizer. Nearly 20 percent of U.S. waste is burned, and the remaining waste, which makes up about 54 percent, is taken to dumps called landfills.

The Garbage Collector

Once you place your garbage on the curb, it is the responsibility of sanitation workers. They pick up trash all over your city and load it onto garbage trucks.

Most garbage trucks have mechanical arms that pick up trash bins and dumpsters and pour the waste into the truck. Trucks also have machines that smash down waste to make room for more.

recycle — to make used items into new products

compost — a mixture of items that break down; compost is added to soil to make it richer.

17

Aluminum cans can be recycled a limitless number of times.

On a truck, garbage is just starting its journey. Sanitation workers then take the garbage that is already sorted into trash and recyclables to transfer stations. From there, it is sent to landfills or recycling facilities. In some places, sanitation workers drive to a mixed waste processing (MWP) facility. At the facility, workers sort garbage. They pull out waste that can be recycled and send it to recycling centers. The rest of the garbage is sent to landfills.

Workers at Norcal Waste Systems in San Francisco sort up to 2,100 tons (1,900 metric tons) of recyclables per day.

At the Landfill

Today's landfills are not the same as the dumps of long ago. They are no longer holes in the ground where trash piles up.

Modern landfills are carefully designed to protect the area around them. A layer of plastic, clay, or a combination of the two is at the bottom of every landfill. This layer keeps harmful waste from seeping into the ground and damaging the environment.

Workers cover loose garbage with a plastic liner or a heap of soil every day. These steps keep trash from blowing away or affecting nearby wildlife.

EDGE FACT:

No one knows how long it takes plastic containers to break down or if they ever do.

Very little oxygen can get to trash buried in a landfill. Because of this, trash breaks down very slowly.

Choose your compost carefully. Diseased or chemically-treated plants could release harmful substances into the soil.

COMPOSTING BASICS

Burning trash costs nearly twice as much as recycling it. Composting is one great way to recycle trash.

You can compost more trash than you might imagine. Yard clippings, egg cartons, paper towels, fruits, vegetables, and coffee grounds can all be composted.

To try composting, place a mix of these materials in a bin outside your home. Then let the mixture sit and break down.

Your compost is ready when the materials in your bin have turned a dark brown color and they smell like dirt. Use your compost as fertilizer in your garden.

Chapter 4

THE DIRTY TRUTH

Millions of germs lurk around dumpsters.

It's true that waste is gross. Just take a sniff inside a dumpster for proof. But the worst thing about garbage is the effect it has on people and the world around us.

Dangers of Waste

Waste is not just ugly and stinky. It can also be dangerous to your health. When people lived up close and personal with their waste, they caught plagues. Waste can also become harmful over time. Wet waste can develop mold, which can make people sick.

Scientists are well aware of the dangers of dirty living conditions. Houses too filthy for people to live in are **condemned**. People living in them must leave immediately.

condemned – declared unsafe

Trash and the Environment

There are fewer landfills today than there were in the past. But these landfills are enormous compared to the landfills of long ago. Overall, the amount of landfill space has remained almost the same.

Landfills keep trash away from where people live. But the areas surrounding these landfills are often in danger. Fumes from the landfills can be dangerous for people or animals that breathe them.

Some studies have shown that as many as 82 percent of landfills have leaks. This means that hazardous waste is leaking into the soil, air, and water surrounding the landfills. These leaks could have terrible effects on the surrounding wildlife.

Wild animals can get sick after eating rotten, dirty food from landfills.

What You Can Do

Believe it or not, you play an important role in trash management. How much you throw away and where you throw it affects the amount of trash in landfills.

Scientists estimate that nearly 90 percent of all waste is recyclable. It's easy to remember to recycle aluminum, but don't forget about plastic and cardboard. Remember to recycle your unwanted mail and other papers.

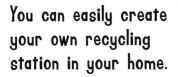
You can easily create your own recycling station in your home.

You might also consider reusable options for disposable items like cups, napkins, and paper bags. Buy recycled gift wrap and gift bags. Small steps can make a huge impact, especially when they are made by many people.

EDGE FACT:

The average U.S. citizen uses seven trees worth of paper products per year.

GLOSSARY

compost (KOM-pohst) — a mixture of rotted leaves, vegetables, manure, and other items that are added to soil to make it richer

condemned (kuhn-DEMD) — declared unsafe

hazardous waste (HAZ-ur-duhss WAYST) — dangerous materials that need to be disposed of safely

incinerator (in-SIN-uh-ray-tur) — a furnace for burning garbage and other waste materials

plague (PLAYG) — a serious disease that spreads quickly to many people and often causes death

recycle (ree-SYE-kuhl) — to make used items into new products; people can recycle items such as rubber, glass, plastic, and aluminum.

toxic (TOK-sik) — poisonous

READ MORE

Inskipp, Carol. *Reducing and Recycling Waste.* Improving Our Environment. Milwaukee: Gareth Stevens, 2005.

Koontz, Robin Michal. *Composting: Nature's Recyclers.* Amazing Science. Minneapolis: Picture Window Books, 2007.

Wilcox, Charlotte. *Recycling.* Cool Science. Minneapolis: Lerner, 2008.

INTERNET SITES

FactHound offers a safe, fun way to find Internet sites related to this book. All of the sites on FactHound have been researched by our staff.

Here's how:
1. Visit *www.facthound.com*
2. Choose your grade level.
3. Type in this book ID **1429619961** for age-appropriate sites. You may also browse subjects by clicking on letters, or by clicking on pictures and words.
4. Click on the **Fetch It** button.

FactHound will fetch the best sites for you!

INDEX